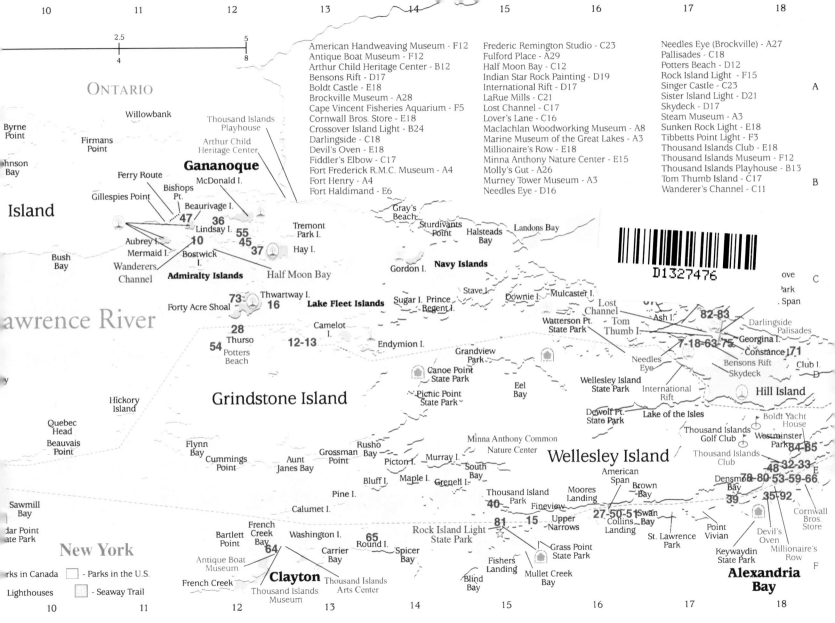

American Handweaving Museum - F12
Antique Boat Museum - F12
Arthur Child Heritage Center - B12
Bensons Rift - D17
Boldt Castle - E18
Brockville Museum - A28
Cape Vincent Fisheries Aquarium - F5
Cornwall Bros. Store - E18
Crossover Island Light - B24
Darlingside - C18
Devil's Oven - E18
Fiddler's Elbow - C17
Fort Frederick R.M.C. Museum - A4
Fort Henry - A4
Fort Haldimand - E6

Frederic Remington Studio - C23
Fulford Place - A29
Half Moon Bay - C12
Indian Star Rock Painting - D19
International Rift - D17
LaRue Mills - C21
Lost Channel - C17
Lover's Lane - C16
Maclachlan Woodworking Museum - A8
Marine Museum of the Great Lakes - A3
Millionaire's Row - E18
Minna Anthony Nature Center - E15
Molly's Gut - A26
Murney Tower Museum - A3
Needles Eye - D16

Needles Eye (Brockville) - A27
Pallisades - C18
Potters Beach - D12
Rock Island Light - F15
Singer Castle - C23
Sister Island Light - D21
Skydeck - D17
Steam Museum - A3
Sunken Rock Light - E18
Tibbetts Point Light - F3
Thousand Islands Club - E18
Thousand Islands Museum - F12
Thousand Islands Playhouse - B13
Tom Thumb Island - C17
Wanderer's Channel - C11

The very best of Ian Coristine's

1000
Islands

I was here once as a toddler, but the only faint memory that remains is a child's fascination with fish swimming in a boathouse. It was almost forty years before I returned. My business had been the distribution of Challenger recreational aircraft in Canada. Flying them, I have enjoyed many "privileged view" low and slow tours of the countryside, including several north-south trips across the U.S., but with a plane on wheels, water is not a place to linger.

That changed in 1992 when I set off on a mini-vacation with two friends, each of us flying our own float-equipped Challengers. The intent, now that we were "boat" owners, was to explore some of eastern Canada's waterways, of which I knew very little. Shortly after takeoff, we crossed the St. Lawrence. By chance, I happened to turn right, following it upstream from my home near Montreal. It was an interesting but not exceptional experience until we reached Brockville, where very suddenly the River changed dramatically.

I was astonished by a labyrinth of exquisite granite and pine islands set in clear, green water. The more we explored, the more profound the experience. It was a day of wonder, rich in wildlife and natural beauty while shipwrecks in the shallows, old lighthouses, cottages, yacht houses and even castles suggested a fascinating history.

A quest began and three years later, I became the owner of a small island, quite literally one in a thousand because it alone offers perfect shelter for my plane from marauding storms. Its natural harbor is exactly a wingspan wide and at the end, a sloping lawn allows me to taxi onto dry land to a perfectly protected tie-down.

It mystifies me that like so many others, I had lived within an easy drive of the area, yet never realized what was here. My photography began as an attempt to show friends what I had "discovered," but I soon realized a number of unlikely ingredients had converged to present an opportunity. I had become comfortable using a camera while flying, through many years of air-to-air photography. I owned the perfect plane for the task and unlike most photographers who are expected to capture the spirit of a place in a brief visit, I was living in the assignment. If the magic didn't cooperate today, I could try again tomorrow, or the next day, week, month or year.

I began to realize this was more than an opportunity, it was an obligation. If I didn't do this, it was very unlikely these ingredients would come together again. The result is a library of over 30,000 images acquired over fifteen years and counting, the very best of which I am proud to share here.

4 B-24 A seemingly simple photograph of my favorite place, equally viewable right side up or upside down. The challenge was to keep the canoe still enough to let the ripples dissipate while holding this vantage point in a slight current, a task that took almost an hour to accomplish.

Power boats are a must in the 1000 Islands, but the slower pace of a rowing skiff, canoe or kayak is the best way to fully appreciate the islands' beauty. While similar in makeup, each is remarkably different and from each the River appears to be an entirely different place.

In 1848, Crossover Island Lighthouse began warning ships away from a line of shoals at a place where the shipping channel crosses over from the Canadian shore to the U.S. mainland. Decommissioned in 1942, the keeper's house now serves as a private residence.

I'm often asked about my favorite camera. The answer is: "Whatever is with me when I need it." For exactly this reason I almost always carry a

pocket camera when my camera bag is left behind. This spring moment in the Lost Channel shows the rewards.

Quiet dawns bring River music: a flock of Canada Geese honking excitedly, loons wailing back and forth while seagulls squabble over breakfast. On the island, waves rhythmically begin breaking, seemingly out of nowhere, precisely twelve minutes after a ship has passed.

I love loons, but find them challenging to photograph, particularly while respecting their privacy as they are easily stressed. I had always hoped to photograph a mother carrying her baby. Three seasons after a family began nesting on a nearby island, the opportunity finally came.

Captain William Fitzwilliam Owen named many of the over one hundred islands in this group off Gananoque after members of the British Admiralty following the War of 1812. Today the Admiralties offer sailors a protected and beautiful anchorage not far from open sailing waters.

Daybreak in late fall occasionally finds the River cloaked in sea smoke as the water releases summer's accumulated warmth into suddenly colder air, as though preparing these Chippewa Bay Islands for Halloween.

I was formation flying with another Challenger as part of a History Channel documentary about ultralight aircraft when this magical scene appeared in the Lake Fleet Islands. A frustrated cameraman in the other plane couldn't understand why I bolted until he later saw this shot.

Frederick Bourne was the wealthiest of the summer people. When Singer sewing machines were slow sellers at $42, he devised an innovative payment plan of a dollar a week and then multiplied the formula around the globe to build one of the world's first multinational corporations.

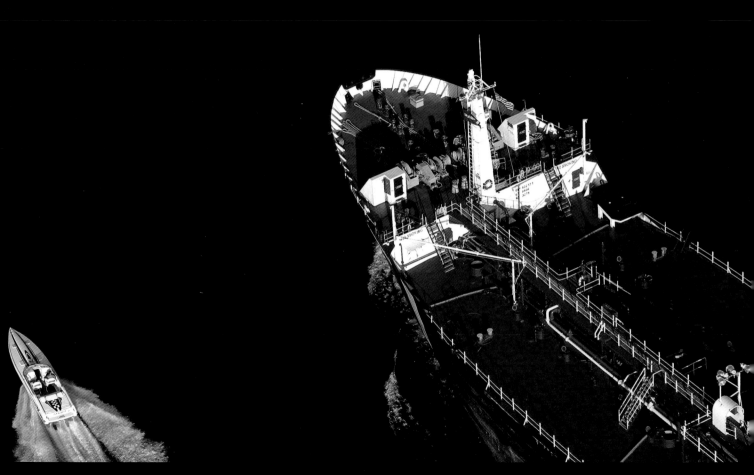

A fascinating marine display sets life on the River apart from life on a lake. On any given day, it can offer up anything from a tall ship to giant lakers and everything in between. Any ship from around the world that can make it through the Seaway's 766 by 80-foot locks is a possibility.

16 C-12   This outing had been wasted effort until seconds before sunset. Momentarily, the River came alive with color. The Lake Fleet Islands lie beneath the spotlight with the Admiralties above. Towards the top, a cable ferry connects the thin finger of Bishop's Point to Howe Island.

A rising sun glows in the windows of Dark Island's The Towers, originally built as a "shooting box" by Singer Sewing Machine's president Frederick Gilbert Bourne. That's what he told his family he'd built, until they rounded Cedar Island in 1905 for their first visit.

Fishing was the initial draw to the region in the mid-1800s and remains significant today, with muskie the most prized catch. Conservation-minded fishermen now practice catch and release so weights are an estimate, but late in 2008, Forty Acre Shoal produced a 57-inch monster.

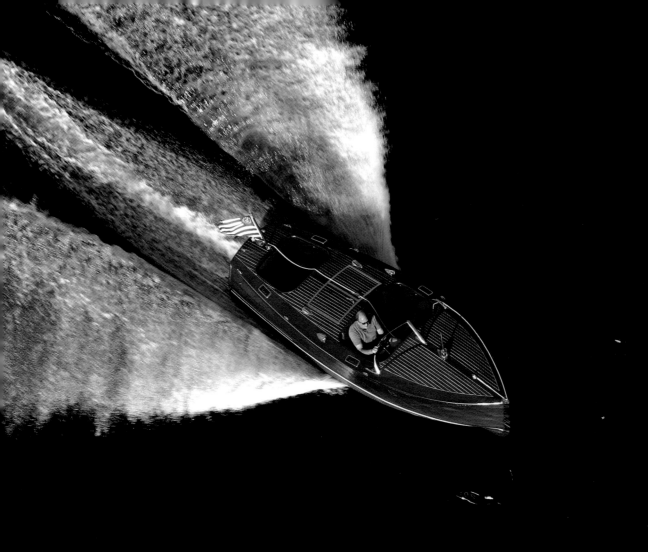

This islander lingered with curiosity while I fueled my plane at a Rockport marina. When he left, I waited for his wake to dissipate before taking off, by chance exactly long enough to pop over the next island to discover him carving the early morning's glassy calm beyond.

Dawn moments like this are fleeting. Typically, by the time my camera and tripod are ready, they are faded or gone. Fortunately, on this morning all I needed was to steady my camera on the windowsill and squeeze the shutter without even getting out of bed.

There are those who insist that to qualify as an island, it must be above water year-round as well as have two trees. Others suggest one is sufficient. I planted a pair of rare pitch pines on this rock. Only one survived, so you make the call. Regardless, over 1,800 others make the cut.

Thunderstorms offer wonderful entertainment, but I find them ridiculously challenging to photograph. I now have an electronic device which helps, but this shot came the old-fashioned way. It took many storms, hundreds of shots and more than a few soakings before I finally got lucky. My Irish Setter watches the show.

The pink granite of the islands, roots of ancient mountains of the Frontenac Arch, is amongst the oldest exposed rock in the world. As the inland sea drained following the Ice Age, less resistant rock and sediment eroded, leaving behind 1,865 jewels, all cherished by islanders.

24 B-25   Fog on the River paints magical scenes, but not without danger. It was thicker than this on the 18th of March, 1991 when *CCGS Griffon* collided with the fishing vessel *Captain K*, sending her and a crew of three to the bottom.

In the mid-1800s, the baby daughter of Crossover Island's lighthouse keeper fell gravely ill. When all conventional treatment failed, a passing Indian woman selling sweetgrass baskets offered help. With her intensive care and potion of wild herbs, the baby miraculously recovered.

Asa Packer knew that if he could get Pennsylvania coal to market, he'd make a fortune. After his Lehigh Canal was destroyed by floods in 1841, he succeeded in building the Lehigh Valley Railroad. The iron bridge was built in 1880 to link two family islands, Sport and Little Lehigh.

With a road deck 150 feet above the water, the U.S. Span was designed to provide clearance for naval ships, despite the fact the St. Lawrence Seaway that would bring them here was no more than a concept when the bridge opened in 1938.

Mist offers wonderful photo opportunities such as here at Grindstone Island, but fog is not something to be trifled with in an airplane. I've seen conditions change almost instantly, so before flying into such situations I carefully survey my landing options.

This morning looks golden-glow warm, but it's precisely because it's so cold that sea smoke is rising. The challenge after a couple of hours of leaning into the slipstream is warming up, a problem solved beautifully after I invested in a small hot tub.

Tibbetts Point Lighthouse has stood guard at the point where Lake Ontario flows into the St. Lawrence River ever since the original light was erected in 1827. The green-roofed building houses a pair of steam foghorns. Locals celebrate the fact that they are no longer used.

Old charts used the name Three Sisters, though today it is known as Sister Island. The explanation came when I purchased a sketch dated 1870, the year the lighthouse was built. It revealed three individual islands joined by bridges. The gaps were later filled, creating a single island.

32 E-18   A ninety-foot clock and bell tower crowns the building which provided electrical power to Heart Island long before it was commonly available on shore. Fifteen bells ranging in size from twelve to fourteen feet were intended to be played from a keyboard in the main castle.

George Boldt envisioned Alster Tower with its bowling alleys, billiard room, library, café-grill, performing stage and a shell-shaped room for dancing as the playhouse. It was the only building actually completed and occupied by the family before the island was abandoned in 1904.

When Arthur Hagan married his laundress Emma, she became one of the resort's socialites, hosting galas in the upstairs ballroom of their Ina Island boathouse. Later, the island gained a somewhat different reputation when it served as a brothel.

An incredible amount of TLC is invested in the restoration of antique boats on the River, so it is of little surprise that similar efforts are expended on some of their boathouses, like this showpiece on Cherry Island.

Kingston's *Canadian Empress* is the only ship offering overnight cruises within the 1000 Islands. Styled after classic River steamships of the 1800s, her passenger list often includes returnees who find the experience sufficiently compelling to have cruised with her dozens of times.

Some of the most delightful islands are amongst the smallest. Location, location, location as always, matters. Despite diminutive size, the right setting such as here in the Admiralties, offers extraordinary views of one of the world's most unique and beautiful archipelagos.

A few marinas on the River offer houseboats for rent for a very different cottage experience. On the nearby Rideau Waterway where they are also popular, it is said that a boater's greatest fear is to be cornered in a lock when a novice houseboater barges in.

Comfort Island's Neh Mahbin was built in 1893 by stockbroker James Oliphant after a fire destroyed the original cottage. Oliphant was murdered in 1907 by a despondent client who had suffered major losses during a financial panic.

T. I. Park's pavilion was an important stop for steamboats bringing guests to the Thousand Island Park Hotel and later to the palatial Columbian. It remains a focus of life in the Park despite passenger service ending after both hotels were lost to fire in 1890 and 1911, respectively.

A favorite for visitors on tour boats which pass on the other side, Zavikon Island is known to millions as having the world's shortest international bridge, joining the cottage in Canada to its backyard in the U.S.

Royal Military College, Canada's West Point, occupies a peninsula where the Royal Naval Dockyards once built warships for use on Lake Ontario because rapids downstream prevented the fleet from reaching the lakes. Kingston, Ontario's historic Limestone City, lies beyond.

44 A-27 Many of the original cottages on the River have been demolished to make way for more substantial homes, but not all succeed in capturing the
appeal of what they replaced. Fortunately, this gem at Fernbank in the Brockville Narrows still exudes all of its Victorian charm.

Books from the 19th century referred to the 1000 Islands as the "Venice of America," which was not much of an exaggeration. Earlier still, travelers carefully followed routes close to shore marked with fast growing poplar trees for fear of becoming lost forever in the maze.

46 C-5   I didn't know where to turn to find out how an extensive network of saw-toothed channels came to be near Wolfe Island's Bayfield Bay. Eventually I learned they were carved by "Ducks Unlimited Canada" to increase secluded breeding areas for territorial waterfowl.

The classic granite and pine islands are part of the Frontenac Arch, a geological bridge which connects the Canadian Shield to the Adirondacks.   B-11 **47**
From Howe Island (left) westwards, the islands are sedimentary rock, the ancient bottom of an inland sea compressed by mile-high glaciers.

When contractor Seth Pope excavated for the original cottage on Nobby Island in 1884, he discovered six human skeletons. They were reburied elsewhere with no investigation permitted. The episode remains a mystery. No additional skeletons were unearthed with this recent addition.

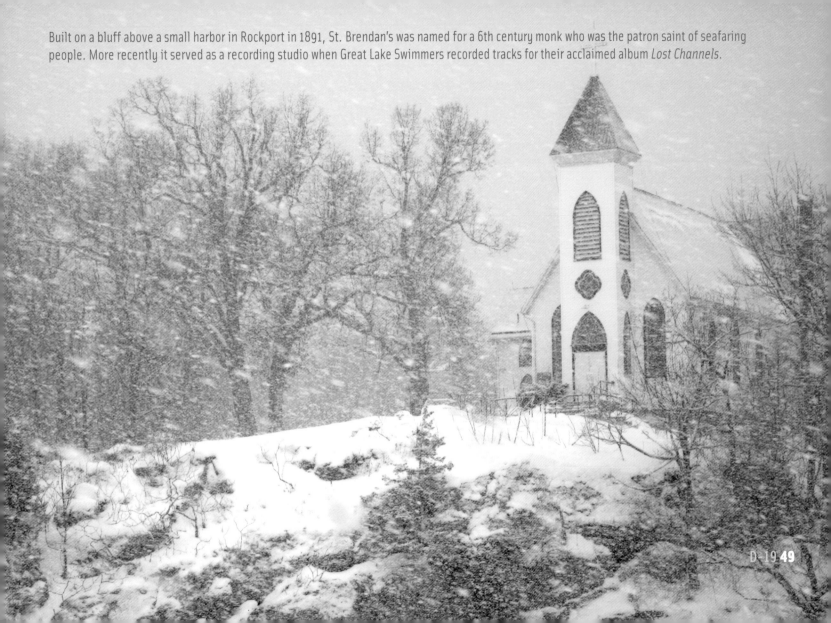

Built on a bluff above a small harbor in Rockport in 1891, St. Brendan's was named for a 6th century monk who was the patron saint of seafaring people. More recently it served as a recording studio when Great Lake Swimmers recorded tracks for their acclaimed album *Lost Channels*.

50 F-16   I had almost turned for home on this morning because fog persisted on the River, but I've learned not to give up too quickly. Rewards often come when you least expect them, as happened here at the U.S. Span when I found myself alone in the sky with this truck.

If this image included a soundtrack, you'd be listening to the deafening bellow of this ship's foghorn waking the River, which the helmsman in the centre window of the bridge is blowing aggressively.

Rt. Hon. PAUL J. MARTIN

Underwater much of the year, islands grow in size as the River's level falls late in the season. While there is a natural seasonal variation, levels are primarily controlled by two huge dams that lie between Cornwall, Ontario and Massena, New York which hold back Lake Ontario.

Predawn takeoffs make it impossible to know if the light or mood will cooperate, but mist on this morning offered promise. As daylight grew, I was dismayed to find most of the River smothered in fog. I persisted and eventually the sun burned through in exactly the right place.

E-18 **53**

There are a great many places to enjoy the River, but not many beaches. Grindstone Island's Potter's Beach has been a favorite for generations, now protected forever under the stewardship of the Thousand Islands Land Trust.

Ynesgrag or Ynys-craig as it is spelled in Welsh means "house on a rock" or in this case two rocks or tiny islands with a seven-room cottage spanning the gap, thus providing indoor parking for family boats.

Capt. T. G. Fuller, one of Canada's most decorated naval heros, designed and built the 125-foot *Fair Jeanne* and named her for his wife, a wise move given that she was built in the backyard. Completed at the age of 73, he then sailed her some 100,000 miles revisiting wartime haunts.

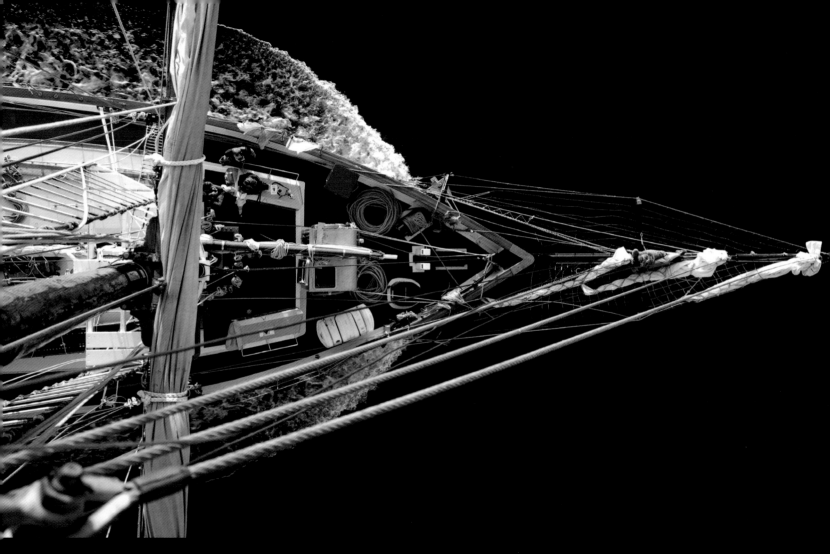

Bytown Brigantine operates two tall ships, *Black Jack* and *Fair Jeanne* as adventure/sail training camps afloat, building character in youth and adults alike as this view from *Fair Jeanne*'s rigging readily attests. An off-duty crew member enjoys some R&R and the view from the bowsprit.

58 E-6   Philo Remington, president of Remington Arms, summered modestly at T.I. Park while his super typewriter salesman William O. Wyckoff built Carleton Villa, one of the first castles in 1894. After years of construction, W.O. moved in to enjoy his first night but never woke in the morning.

After Louise Boldt's death in 1904, George Boldt abandoned his castle and the building began seventy-three years of deterioration. Thanks to the vision of the Thousand Islands Bridge Authority, it was rescued from a fate which has claimed a number of other gilded age treasures.

The elderly couple who preceded me at the island advised, "This is a green leaf place. Whenever the leaves are green there is no place in the

I am constantly drawn to this grouping of islands in Chippewa Bay, shaped by glaciers to look like a convoy of ships on a golden sea. Bluff Island in the foreground is actually two islands joined by a cottage which provides convenient sheltered dockage for boats beneath.

When the St. Lawrence Seaway's route was planned in the 1950s, good fortune squeezed it through a tight passage in the Brockville Narrows, emerging very close to the downtown waterfront. Brockvillians have been treated to an entertaining maritime spectacle ever since.

On August 14, 1760, Britain's *HMS Onondaga* was lured into the labyrinth by French attackers. A boat with 14 men was lowered to warn *HMS Mohawk* away, but was never seen again. On failing to find even where it was lowered, this spot became known as the Lost Channel.

64 F-12   When the Iroquois Confederacy routed an Algonquin stronghold here, this place became known as Fallen Fort. Later it became French Creek before being named Clayton in 1833 after a senator from Delaware who also served as U.S. Secretary of State.

Boats may be a luxury elsewhere, but there's no way to live on an island without at least one and preferably two. Thanks to the encouragement of Clayton's Antique Boat Museum, many islanders own wooden works of art like this 1931 Hutchinson at Round Island's post office.

Sometimes it takes fresh eyes to see what's buried in the library. I passed over this for years until a magazine asked to use it in a feature. Only through a two-page spread did I see the unlikely scene of a large ship emerging from a labyrinth of islands to stumble upon an island castle

As a child, I occasionally spent weekends with a school friend whose family owned a large country home on a private lake in Quebec's Laurentians. It wasn't their rambling cottage that became my ideal, but a tiny guesthouse built on the dock, very reminiscent of this.

Great Lake Swimmers' love affair with the 1000 Islands began while recording their album *Lost Channels* at Singer Castle, Rockport's St. Brendan's Church and Brockville's Arts Centre. *Fair Jeanne* later served as the stage for a concert and music video of their song "Palmistry."

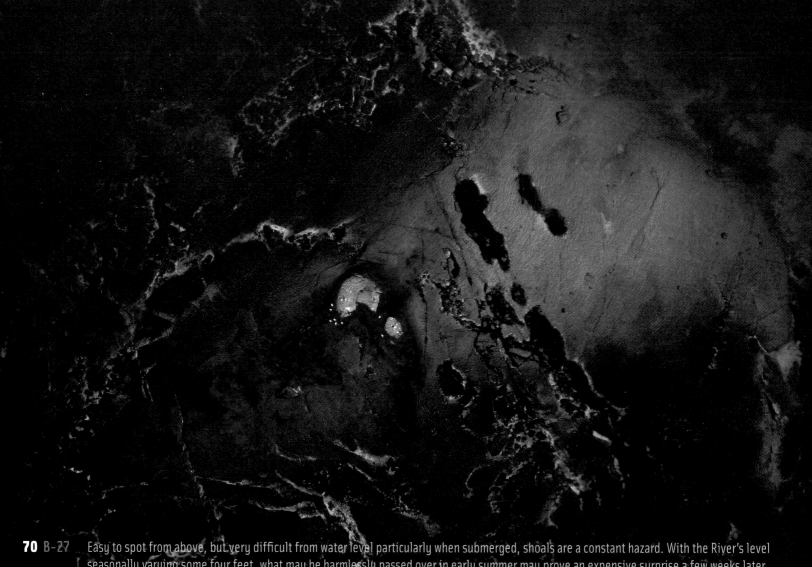

70 B-27   Easy to spot from above, but very difficult from water level particularly when submerged, shoals are a constant hazard. With the River's level seasonally varying some four feet, what may be harmlessly passed over in early summer may prove an expensive surprise a few weeks later.

The quest to own an island encourages ingenuity. Though current regulations no longer permit it, Lone Pine Island is one of several shoals hosting cottages. A few have been enlarged with considerable effort and expense to provide sufficient "land" on which to build.

Grenadier Islanders have a couple of reasons to consider owning a golf cart. A five-mile road and no cars makes them particularly useful. In the 1800s when such conveniences were nonexistent, children here really did have to walk miles through snow drifts to get to and from school.

Conceived in the 1870s, St. Lawrence Islands is one of Canada's oldest, most beautiful and unique national parks, composed of over twenty magnificent islands. Thwartway's numerous bays and protected coves make it a particularly popular retreat in the Lake Fleet Group.

Sunken Rock Light guards the east end of the American Narrows, but in 1974 the 641-foot *Roy A. Jodrey* struck a buoy here and began taking on water. Intentionally run aground on Pullman Shoal, she began a slide down its steep slope that didn't stop until she reached the bottom.

The 1000 Islands are blessed with two majestic bridges which compliment the area's natural beauty rather than detracting from it. This one is the Canadian Span which uses three separate sections, touching down on three islands to reach the Canadian mainland.

My son and I watched the *Blue Lady* pass our island, surging and sputtering with an apparent fuel problem. As she disappeared behind trees, we considered giving chase to offer a tow. Before we could, a loud explosion and thick column of black smoke announced we were too late.

The 1000 Islands is said to offer the finest freshwater diving in the world. The attraction is countless well preserved shipwrecks, like the *Pentland* and *F. A. Georger* which lie together in a shallow bay on Grenadier Island's south shore near Sister Island Lighthouse.

In 1888, George Pullman's Castle Rest was the first of the great castles, but was demolished when shortsighted officials refused tax abatement despite post-depression realities. The village lost both an historic landmark and its taxes, leaving only the powerhouse and outbuildings.

DDT ravaged Osprey populations such that by 1992, only a single nesting pair remained in the 1000 Islands. Nesting platforms were erected with such success that the birds began using navigational aids, requiring the Coast Guard to erect taller platforms nearby to lure them away.

B-24 79

Hopewell Hall was built by William Browning who made his fortune supplying uniforms during the Civil War. One of many homes purchased by George Boldt, it became his daughter Clover's. She removed several dormers and towers to simplify it, preferring a less ostentatious display

Following a career of piracy which included robbing and sinking the steamer *Sir Robert Peel* immediately downstream of Rock Island Light in 1838, Bill Johnston was jailed but eventually pardoned. In 1852, he returned to begin a more sedate career as its first keeper.

82 C-17 Backlighting often reveals an enchanting world. Moments before, I shot the bridge from the sunny side with postcard style results. Only when I looked back into the sunrise did the clouds come alive, glowing colorfully against silhouetted islands.

84 E-18   At the turn of the century, dozens of steam yachts similar to the 62-foot *Kestrel* were owned by islanders with fourteen over 100 feet in length. George Boldt had sixty boats ranging from his 104-foot houseboat *La Duchesse* to a series of racing boats named *PDQ - Pretty Damned Quick.*

Early in the 20th century, an effort was made to purchase Boldt Castle and Heart Island for use as a permanent summer White House for Woodrow Wilson and future Presidents. Funding failed to materialize when Word War I intervened.

Calm, clear and sunny on shore, the first deep freeze of the season transforms the River into writhing sea smoke as the water crystallizes into a sheet of ice.

I find that worthy images of specific subjects almost never come on demand, so I try to keep an open mind and look for what might be found. On this morning I was focusing on Singer Castle, only to turn around to discover the magic was happening right behind me.

88 C-23   Like many dawn sorties, this one seemed wasted effort when cloud cover proved more extensive than expected. Occasional holes appeared near Chippewa Bay so I guesstimated Singer Castle's position, circling almost until fuel exhaustion. A momentary hole appeared just in time.

Of the great castles - Carleton Villa, Calumet Castle, Castle Rest, Boldt Castle - only Frederick Bourne's Singer Castle made it into the appreciative hands of the next generation. Marjorie Bourne loved and even expanded her father's dream, but the era ended with her passing.

My friend Paul Malo returned with me to the island on a foggy evening after the opening of an exhibition we presented together at St. Lawrence University in Canton, NY. The instant he saw this image, he titled it "Sunken Cathedral," which captures it perfectly.

Local legend tells of a chest carrying the payroll lost in Jones Creek during a War of 1812 skirmish. In 1908, a resident invested in a barge, dredging unsuccessfully but leaving behind a mound of rubble. A willow twig rooted and ever since has served as Toniata Island's only tree.

Great friends and business partners, Nathan Strauss and Abraham Abraham built a pair of mirror image cottages, Belora and Olympia at the

Brockville, one of Canada's finest small cities as well as Ontario's oldest, is the eastern gateway to the region. Settled by Loyalists after the revolution, it boasts a treasure trove of historic homes, 16 park islands, an exquisite 150-year-old theater and a fascinating nautical parade

While these islands may seem unremarkable; 1000 Islanders instantly recognize only one place in the world looks quite like this. Rare pitch pines, multi-hued lichens smothering pink granite and seaweed bleaching as the water level drops tells them this can only be "The River."

This is the dining room. As I explain to guests, the island and view are the attractions with the cottage simply offering shelter and facilities for cooking and sleeping. Mother Nature has done a far better job of decorating than I ever could, so I do as little as possible to interfere.

When I published my first book of photography in 2002, I had no idea if anyone would care enough to buy it, much less that eight years later I'd be releasing a fifth volume. The only reason it happened is because of the amazing encouragement and support I have received from so many, not least the shop owners and islanders who share my love for this place. Room won't allow mentioning all who helped, but I would like to single out a few: DxO Labs of Paris, France, whose software allows my cameras and lenses to be technically flawless, Hayley, Mary and Scotty Coristine, Simon Fuller, Dave Goulet, Michael Keyser, Andy Li, Kim Lunman, Dave O'Malley, Joan Michie, Terry Page and Susan Smith.

It is more than appropriate that a compilation of my best work be dedicated to my much missed best friend, Paul Malo, who showed me through years of encouragement just how important a role a truly great professor can play in one's life. His legacy continues through the online magazine he founded: www.thousandislandslife.com.

Images from the books are available as high quality giclée prints suitable for framing. Each is reproduced on acid-free paper using archival inks and is titled and signed by the artist. Wholesale pricing is available for volume orders for businesses wishing to decorate relevantly, including framing as required. Complimentary screen-saver images of the 1000 Islands intended to alleviate winter withdrawal are also available. Subscribe at Notification List under Contact at: www.1000islandsphotoart.com.

Library and Archives Canada Cataloguing in Publication
Coristine, Ian, 1949-
The very best of Ian Coristine's 1000 Islands

ISBN 978-0-9730419-6-5

1) Thousand Islands (NY. and Ont.)--Aerial photographs.
2. Thousand Islands (N.Y. and Ont.)--Pictorial works.
I. Title. II. Title: Thousand Islands V.
FC3095.T43C677 2010   971.3'7050222   C2009-907326-9

Published by: 1000 Islands Photo Art Inc. www.1000islandsphotoart.com
Graphic Design by: Aerographics Creative Services (Ottawa, ON) www.aerographics.ca
Printed in China